Bogie

A LIFE IN PICTURES

Judith Schlesinger

MetroBooks

MetroBooks

An Imprint of Friedman/Fairfax Publishers

© 1998 by Michael Friedman Publishing Group, Inc.

Library of Congress Cataloging-in-Publication data
available upon request.

ISBN 1-56799-617-5

Editor: Francine Hornberger
Art Director: Jeff Batzli
Designer: Charles Donahue
Photography Editor: Sarah Storey
Production Manager: Ingrid Neimanis-McNamara

Color separations by HBM Print Ltd.
Printed in China by Leefung-Asco Printers Ltd.

1 3 5 7 9 10 8 6 4 2

For bulk purchases and special sales, please contact:
Friedman/Fairfax Publishers
Attention: Sales Department
15 West 26th Street
New York, NY 10010
212/685-6610   FAX 212/685-1307

Visit our website:
http://www.metrobooks.com

Acknowledgments

Many thanks to those who made this book possible and such fun to write: Steve Slaybaugh, Francine Hornberger, Emily Zelner, Sarah Storey, and Ms. Pumps (a.k.a. Carol Krenz).

Dedication

To my three heroes:
Joe Schlesinger, Bill Sieland, and Rich Miller

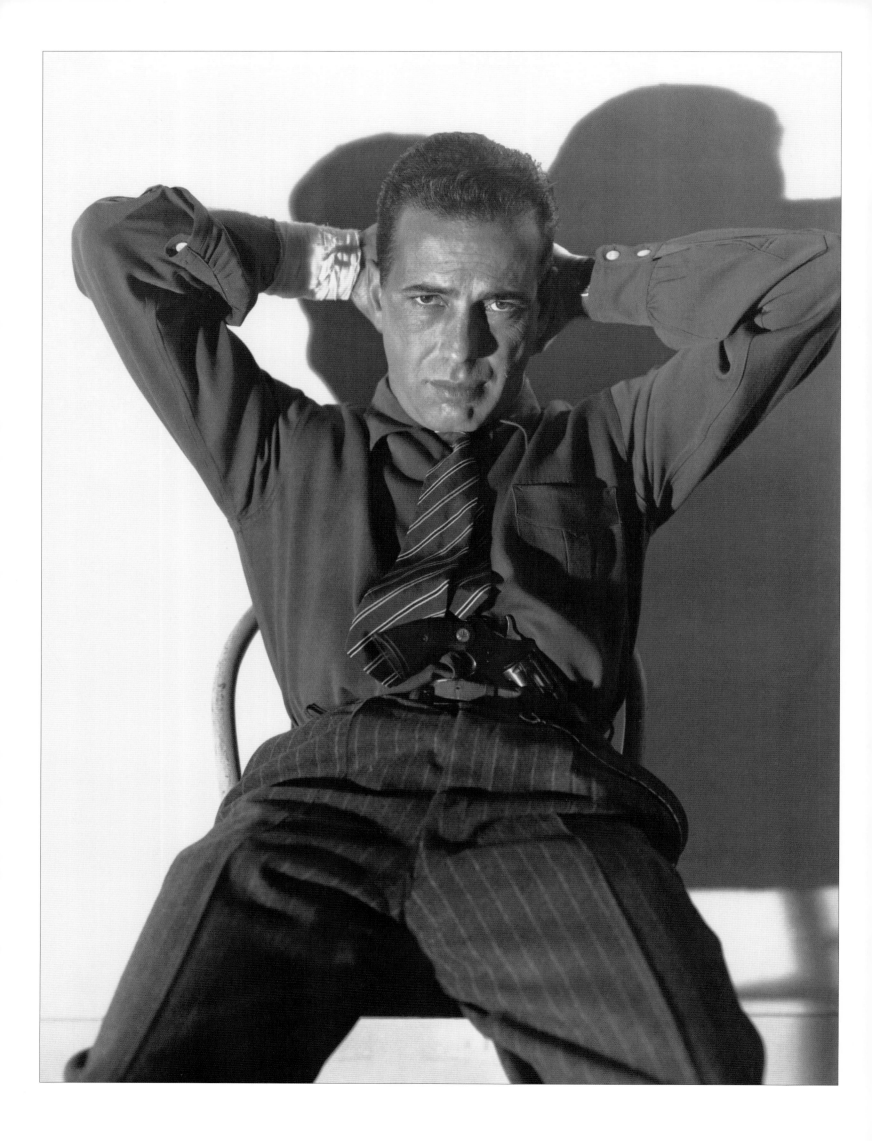

CONTENTS

Introduction

Opposite: Bogie on the *Sierra* set with "Pard" (actually his own pet, Zero), the mutt whose bark reveals Mad Dog's hiding place to the police and results in his eighty-nine-foot (27m) climactic slide down the mountain. Buster Wiles, the stuntman who doubled for Bogie, wanted another take because he'd bounced a few times. "Forget it," said director Walsh. "It's good enough for the 25-cent customers."

Above: Bogie as "Mad Dog" Roy Earle in *High Sierra* (1941), a breakthrough film for him. Producers Hal Wallis and Mark Hellinger and director Raoul Walsh, along with fine writing by John Huston, combined to create an exciting action film and one of Bogie's most memorable roles.

Painful childhoods do not create talent, but they can shape its expression. It's likely that Bogie's trademark cynicism, his mistrust of authority, and his allergy to phonies began with his early lessons in the gap between appearance and reality.

Humphrey DeForest Bogart arrived on Christmas Day, 1899, the first child of Dr. Belmont DeForest Bogart, a surgeon, and Maud Humphrey, the most famous children's illustrator of her time. The Bogarts lived on the fashionable Upper West Side of Manhattan and summered at their Victorian "cottage" in upstate New York. To the world, theirs was a genteel, upper-middle-class existence; to Bogie and his sisters, it was a private nightmare of marital screaming, neglect, and abusive servants, complicated by the drinking and morphine addiction of both parents. Maud drew tender portraits of babies even as she rejected her own. In a 1949 article titled "I Can't Say I Loved Her," Bogie said, "She was totally incapable of showing affection to us." The "us" included Kay (Catty), who died at thirty-four from peritonitis complicated by alcoholism, and Francis Rose (Pat), who broke down after twenty-seven hours in childbirth and whose lifelong treatment was financed by her brother. Despite his mother's neglect, Bogie took her in after his father died, exhibiting the sense of duty that characterized his personal life—and motivated his greatest characters.

Young Bogart had to fight to prove he wasn't a sissy, despite his funny name and the Little Lord Fauntleroy outfits Maud forced him to wear. This ended in adolescence, when he grew into a good-looking ringleader called "Hump." (He didn't become "Bogie" until 1930, when Spencer Tracy gave him the nickname.) An indifferent student who got the worst grades at the best schools, he later educated himself through voracious reading and became close friends with some of America's leading writers.

Expelled from Andover in 1918, Bogie joined the Naval Reserve, skipping the shipyard job his family had arranged for him. Honorably discharged in 1919, he drifted for two years through a series of menial jobs. But his inner current was steadily moving him toward acting, and once he made his professional debut—playing a Japanese butler in a 1921 Brooklyn play—he never drifted again.

Opposite: By 1942—even before *Casablanca* was released—75 percent of Bogie's fan mail was from women. Typically, he scoffed at his sexy image: "I don't like [love scenes], maybe because I don't do them very well. It isn't possible to shoot [them] without having a hairy-chested group of grips standing four feet [1.2m] away from you, chewing tobacco. I'll handle that in the privacy of my bedroom, old boy."

Below: Bogie on the set of *The Treasure of the Sierra Madre* (1948). Robert Blake (later known as television's Baretta) played a street kid in the film and remembers: "He was not like other actors. It was almost like he was the prop man—very quiet, but also the center of things. You knew that when you were near him you were safe." With the exception of his firestorms with his third wife, Mayo Methot during the filming of earlier movies, Bogie's conduct on set was always professional.

From 1922 to 1935 Bogie appeared in twenty-one Broadway productions. At five feet nine inches (175cm) and 155 pounds (70kg), he got what he called "White Pants Willie" roles, where his usual purpose onstage was to swing a tennis racket and announce a game. During this period, Bogie's first two marriages began and dissolved. Helen Menken (married 1926–1927) and Mary Philips (married 1928–1937) were both talented, independent, and volatile actresses with temper and/or alcohol problems. But they were lambs compared to wife number three, Mayo Methot (married 1938–1945). She was half of "the battling Bogarts," known for their drunken public brawling and mutual black eyes. Mayo was succeeded by Bogie's last wife, Lauren Bacall, who became his widow twelve years later.

Bogie's introduction to Hollywood foreshadowed his later frustration: the studios wanted him, but kept assigning him dumb roles in mediocre films. His first contract, with the Fox Film Corporation, ended in 1931 after six duds. Married at the time to Mary Philips, whose career had taken off in New York, Bogie moved from Broadway to Hollywood several times before he finally settled in California.

His big break came with The Petrified Forest, Sherwood Anderson's 1934 hit play in which Bogie played escaped killer Duke Mantee to enthusiastic reviews. Warner Brothers bought the rights, planning to cast Edward G. Robinson for the movie role, but Leslie Howard—who played the dreamy poet in both versions—refused to make the film without Bogie. His simmering Mantee garnered Bogie a Best Supporting Actor nomination and a contract with Warners. At the age of thirty-five, after twelve years in show business, he was an overnight sensation.

But even this success didn't assure his position. After The Petrified Forest, he suffered a long dry spell: twenty-five unexceptional films between 1936 and 1939 were mostly gangster flicks in which he played "Bugs" or "Rocks" and got killed by the hero. The B movie system was designed for movie quantity, not quality, and Bogie, like other B players, had no vote in the work he would do. The studio assigned him one turkey after another with little, if any, time in between. Refusing a part meant suspension without pay. He could also be "loaned out" to another studio for more than his contracted salary, but Warners pocketed the difference.

Bogie fought this "slave system" until success provided him greater control over his projects. Since he had a knack for picking good screenwriters, his movies improved each time his contracts did. But his need to make a living in the 1930s still propelled him into such embarrassments as a hillbilly musical (Swing Your Lady,

1938) and a vampire flick (The Return of Doctor X, 1939). Most people are surprised to learn that Bogie made seventy-five movies, since his reputation rests on fewer than a dozen.

The post-Forest slump ended in 1941 with Bogie's indelible portraits of "Mad Dog" Roy Earle and Sam Spade in High Sierra and The Maltese Falcon, respectively. George Raft, whose star contract allowed him role refusal, turned down both of these parts—and lived to regret it. With Falcon, Bogie finally got top billing and the chance to kiss the girl, though he had to give her up for reasons of honor—a haunting finale that would later reappear in Casablanca.

Casablanca, 1943's Best Picture, was Bogie's forty-fifth movie and, to many, his finest. It elevated him to sex-symbol status for his darkly romantic portrayal of Rick, the nightclub owner with a mysterious past. Casablanca also finally freed him from B contracts—his next contract with Warners gave him $200,000 per film and a chance to call the shots.

Unfortunately, peaks, by definition, are impossible to sustain. After Casablanca, Bogie made four lesser films: three propaganda pieces and a murder mystery. In late 1943, he and Mayo amused the overseas troops with clips of his many movie deaths, followed by live jokes and songs. Bogie realized that their stormy marriage was also entertaining, but he took the public's curiosity in stride: "I knew that the higher a monkey climbs, the more you can see of his tail."

While 1940s Hollywood did not number sequels as it does today, it used the same hopeful strategy of reproducing the cast, plot, and characters from a previous hit. Many Bogie movies were created this way, taking elements of earlier successes in hopes of borrowing some of their stardust as well. For example, To Have and Have Not (1944) echoed Casablanca: the accidental hero, drawn by personal reasons into risking his life; resistance fighters needing rescue; a significant love song and sympathetic piano player; and another overweight villain (Dan Seymour, replacing Sydney Greenstreet). There was also the lanky, nineteen-year-old Lauren Bacall, making her film debut as "Slim" and becoming the fourth Mrs. Bogie the following year.

With this marriage came children: son Stephen Humphrey Bogart in 1949, named after Bogie's character in the movie that united his parents, and daughter Leslie Howard Bogart in 1952, named for Bogie's friend who protected his breakthrough role as Mantee. When fertility treatments made Bogie's hair fall out, he made fun of his toupees, finding them as amusing as the lifts the studio put in his shoes.

A first-time father at age forty-nine, Bogie was awkward and unsure. "What do you do with a kid?" he said. "They don't drink."

But he did, much too often and often too much. Ever the non-conformist, the only time he refused to get drunk was on New Year's Eve.

While Bacall's movie career soon stalled, Bogie's roles became more interesting. There was his Oscar-winning portrayal of Charlie Allnut, the grizzled, humorous version of Bogie's reluctant hero in *The African Queen* (1951); Linus Larrabee, the lonely workaholic in *Sabrina* (1954); and the unforgettable paranoid Captain Queeg from The *Caine Mutiny* (1954). This was Bogie's last strong movie, though he made six more—the final one ironically called *The Harder They Fall* (1956).

In the mid-1950s, Bogie's happiness was marred by growing health concerns—specifically, a racking cough that began to interfere with filming. His long romance with unfiltered Chesterfields finally caught up with him, but by the time he agreed to see a doctor, it was too late: he had advanced, incurable cancer of the esophagus. Yet even as his body deteriorated, his humor remained intact. In his "Open Letter to the Working Press" he wrote: "I have heard that my heart has...been replaced by an old gasoline pump from a defunct Standard Oil station....All I need now is about thirty pounds [13.5kg] in weight which I'm sure some of you could spare....believe me I'm not particular about which part of your anatomy it comes from."

It took nearly eleven months of wasting away before Bogie died on January 14, 1957, at the age of fifty-seven. John Huston, Bogie's close friend who wrote seven of his movies, ended his eulogy with a reminder that while Bogie's life was far too short, it was a rich and full one—any pity belonged to the survivors for having lost him. "He is quite irreplaceable," Huston said. "There will never be another like him."

Chapter One

Beginnings

Opposite: Humphrey DeForest Bogart, age two. Bogie's childhood was anything but peaceful and happy; the trusting innocence shown in those big brown eyes would not last very long.

Above: The famous sketch by Maud Humphrey that made Bogie the "Gerber baby" of his time when it was bought by the Mellins Baby Food Company. In the early 1900s, Maud made as much as $50,000 a year with her illustrations of children for advertisements and magazine covers. Bogie hated posing for her "pretty" pictures. This, together with his name, curls, and natural tidiness, made him the butt of many schoolyard jokes.

Above: Maud and her firstborn in a rare, if chilly, maternal moment. Both of Bogie's parents abused drugs, alcohol, and their children. In a classic case of trying to win the love he never got from Mom, Bogie was always attracted to Maud-types: feisty, noisy, independent career women who enjoyed a drink and a good fight. As he later said in *High Sierra,* "I wouldn't give you two cents for a dame without a temper."

Below: In 1921, Bogie began his acting career on the stage. Other Hollywood leading men who also got their start on the stage: James Cagney, Spencer Tracy, and Clark Gable. Bogie was usually cast as the juvenile, wearing white flannel pants and swinging a tennis racket. Although he never took any acting classes or had any formal training, Bogie did both dramas and comedies for fourteen years until Hollywood called.

Above: Naval Reserve Seaman Second Class Bogart, age eighteen. One highlight of Bogie's childhood was learning to sail and developing a deep love for the water, which he retained all of his life. The Naval Reserve was a natural choice when he decided to enlist, and after his honorable discharge in 1919, he joined the Coast Guard Reserve as well.

Chapter Two

Broadway and the Early Bs

Opposite: Bogie, circa 1932. By this time, his father had lost both his health and his fortune, and Bogie's one sister was an alcoholic, while the other was mentally ill. His father died in 1934, leaving Bogie $10,000 in debts and a ruby-and-diamond ring that Bogie wore, on and off the screen, for the rest of his life.

Above: Bogie met his first wife, the fiery, successful actress Helen Menken, when they did the play *Drifting* together in 1922. Both twenty-six when they married on May 20, 1926, Bogie and Helen were divorced just over a year later in November 1927. They always remained friends, however, and rekindled their affair occasionally through the years.

Opposite: Bogie and his second wife, Mary Philips, in the 1923 play *Nerves,* where they met; they married in April 1928. Mary, who once bit a cop's finger when he tried to arrest her for drunkenness, would not leave her Broadway stardom to join Bogie in Hollywood while he was trying to break into films. During their separations she claimed, as "a modern couple," they were "both free to date."

Above: Bogie and Ruth Etting in *Like That* (1930), a ten-minute short for Warners that was Bogie's film debut and led to his first contract with Fox. Also featured in the film were Joan Blondell and Bogie's wife, Mary. Distance, career imbalance, and Mary's affair with actor Roland Young all worked to corrode the marriage, which ended in June 1937.

Right: Spencer Tracy meets Bogart in *Up the River* (1930). The movie was forgettable but the friendship was not, enduring for decades until Bogie's death. It was Tracy who first called him "Bogie." During the months that Bogart was dying, Tracy and Katharine Hepburn visited him every day; Tracy was the first choice to give the eulogy, but he was too distraught to do it.

Below: *A Devil with Women* (1930) was Bogie's first full-length picture for Fox. He played a rich young Romeo tagging along with a soldier of fortune (Victor McLaglen) in Central America, where they hunt a bandit and compete for the love of Rosita (Mona Maris, shown). Another minor "White Pants Willie" role—with salsa.

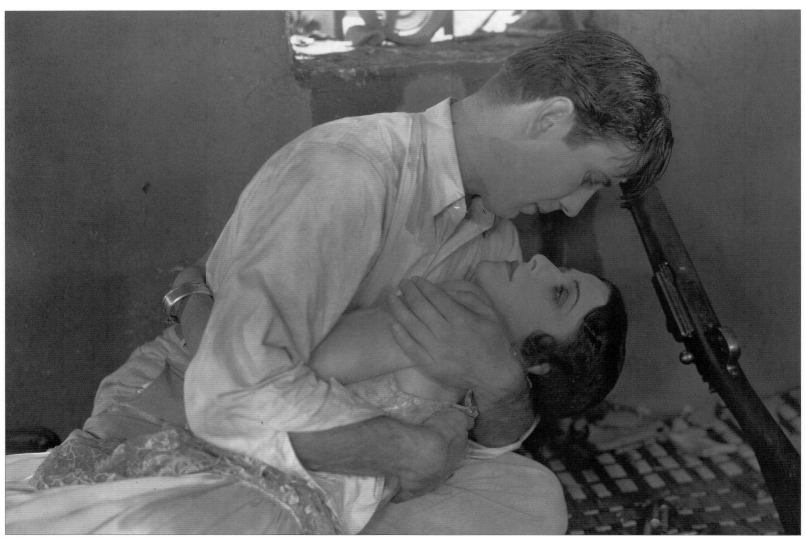

Below: Fox cast Bogie (right) as a daring flyer in *Body and Soul* (1931), but killed him off early in the film. The studio was still having trouble figuring out what to do with him, and "loaned him out" to Universal for his next project.

Above: *Bad Sister* (1931) was Bogie's first picture with Bette Davis; he made more films with her than any other actress. In this film from Universal, he played Valentine Corliss, a smooth swindler who courts Sidney Fox (shown) and disappears halfway through the film—though this time he's alive, and gets to leave with the money.

Right: Back at Fox for *Women of All Nations* (1931), Bogie had a small part as a marine. Bela Lugosi appears as an Egyptian prince with a harem. At this point, Bogie's contract—and patience—with Fox was coming to an end.

Left: In Bogie's last picture for Fox, *A Holy Terror* (1931), he had the third lead as a ranch foreman. His contractual obligation over, Bogie (shown here with Sally Eilers) headed back to Broadway and his wife, Mary. "I guess I was too short to be a cowboy," he said.

Right: After another frustrating shot at Depression-era Broadway—where he made more money playing bridge than acting—Bogie got a six-month contract at Columbia for *Love Affair* (1932), in which he played a flight instructor and inventor who stumbles through a series of romantic misunderstandings until he saves his sweetheart (Dorothy Mackaill) from aerosuicide.

Opposite: Bogie engrossed in a favorite hobby. When the Depression drastically reduced the available work on Broadway, he became the house player at an arcade, earning a dollar a game. Always determined to control his own destiny, chess suited him: "I don't like games based on luck," he said.

Above: Warners became interested in Bogie and offered him a bit part in *Big City Blues* (1932), the story of a small-town boy who goes to New York and attends a wild party where a girl is killed by a flying bottle. The entire action takes place in a seventy-two-hour period; the film's impact on Bogie's career was equally marginal.

Chapter Three

The Forest to the Falcon

Opposite: Bogie played gangster "Rocks" Valentine in *The Amazing Dr. Clitterhouse* (1938), with Edward G. Robinson in the title role. Dr. Clitterhouse is a psychiatrist who studies criminals and who poisons Rocks in order to examine his reaction. A strange story, it was the first Bogie film at least partly written by John Huston, who would later pen some of Bogie's best.

Above: In *King of the Underworld* (1939), Bogie played Joe Gurney, a crime boss with an ego problem who kidnaps a writer to tell his story. Gurney is subdued by a new weapon—blinding eye-drops—administered by a woman doctor whose husband he killed. Shot by police, he says, "Don't tell 'em dat a dame tripped me up!"

Opposite: Bogie and Leslie Howard onstage in *The Petrified Forest* (1934). During each night of the 197 New York performances, Bogie's first appearance made the audience gasp. In the play, Bogart's character, the escaped killer Duke Mantee, gets away—but not in the film. Hollywood's Production Code would never allow a killer to survive. In both play and film, Bogie's and Howard's characters seemed to be opposites, but in fact they were equally desperate, alienated—and doomed.

Above: In the film version of *The Petrified Forest*, Duke Mantee takes over a cafe in the Arizona desert where he meets suicidal poet Alan Squier (Leslie Howard) and Gabrielle (Bette Davis), the girl who dreams of Paris. Warners originally wanted Edward G. Robinson for the role of Mantee, but Howard sent Jack Warner a cable: "NO BOGART NO DEAL."

Right: In *Isle of Fury* (1936) Bogie played Val Stevens, a fugitive living on a South Seas island. Detective Eric Blake (Donald Woods) is sent after him but leaves him alone after some male bonding—Val saves Eric from a shipwreck, and Eric saves Val from an octopus. Critics noted that no movie in which Bogie wore a mustache was ever any good.

Above: Bogie was such a convincing Mantee that he was typecast as a gangster for years. In *Bullets or Ballots* (1936), "Bugs" Fenner (Bogart) meets undercover cop Johnny Blake (Edward G. Robinson) under the suspicious gaze of mobster Al Kruger (Barton MacLane). In the thirty-six films he made between 1932 and 1942, Bogie was arrested or killed in twenty-two: "My principal problem was in finding new ways to say 'Aaaagh' and different ways of spitting blood."

Left: Bogie played Hap Stuart, ace flyer and third lead, in *China Clipper* (1936). While a small role, this was his third incarnation as an expert airman. Audiences were beginning to identify Bogie with cool competence, regardless of which side of the law he happened to be on.

Right: *Black Legion* (1937), a daring, crusading movie, was named for a real racist group in Detroit. Bogie played Frank Taylor, a factory worker who loses his job to a foreigner and joins a secret "pro-American" organization. The film was inspired by the Ku Klux Klan, which sued Warners for "infringement of a design," claiming they held the "patent" on the symbol used for the robes and hoods in the movie. The case was dismissed.

Above: Bogie, Frieda Inescort, and Sybil Jason with Pat O'Brien in the title role of *The Great O'Malley* (1937). The story is a series of improbable plot turns involving a decent father, John Phillips (Bogart), who is "forced" into committing a robbery after his arrest for a minor traffic violation, which makes him miss a job interview, and the small-minded cop who nails him, gets demoted to school crossing guard, and decides to help the family after he meets John's crippled daughter and falls for her teacher.

Opposite, bottom left: There are several theories about how Bogie got his trademark lisp: 1) his father damaged his lip in childhood; 2) he was injured by a flying splinter from an exploding shell in the navy; 3) a prisoner he was transporting smacked him with handcuffs and the navy doctor botched the repair; or 4) he got punched in the mouth at some saloon. No book reveals the "real" story—not even the books by Bacall and their son. It's also possible that Bogie deliberately cultivated his unique speaking style—the rasp, sneer, and twitch—to make himself distinctive.

Left: As real-life killer John Dillinger sparked the character Duke Mantee in *The Petrified Forest,* the film *Marked Woman* (1937) was inspired by "Lucky" Luciano, who ran prostitution rackets in the 1920s and 1930s. District Attorney David Graham (Bogie) tries to mobilize the working girls against their boss. Coyly referred to as "hostesses," the actresses featured included Bette Davis (right) and Bogie's future wife, Mayo Methot (at center, looking fierce).

Above: Mayo Methot, a.k.a. "the Portland Rosebud," was at the peak of her movie career when she met Bogie in 1936. She was also a singer, famous for her rendition of "More Than You Know." Bright, witty, and temperamental, she stirred up Bogie's emotions and, according to one critic, "set fire to his acting." She also set fire to their house during one of her jealous rages.

Above: On August 20, 1938, Bogie and Mayo launched the third marriage for both. Their public fights would become legendary, especially in New York, where they were banned from the posh 21 Club and billed $400 by the Algonquin Hotel for just one night of breakage. They framed the invoice and hung it on their wall.

Left: Bogie visits Mayo on the set. The two shared a robust sense of humor and in the early years were very entertaining, both to their friends and the press. But as Mayo's alcoholism progressed and her career declined, both she and the marriage deteriorated. She even stabbed Bogie in the back once (literally) when she suspected he'd been to a brothel.

Below: *Kid Galahad* (1937) provided a new arena—boxing—but a familiar plot for Bogie. He played a corrupt fight promoter called "Turkey" who tangles with fight manager Nick Donati (Edward G. Robinson). Also rejoining Bogie was Bette Davis, playing Nick's sister, Fluff.

B elow: In *San Quentin* (1937), Bogie played convict "Red" Kennedy, whose sister Mary (Ann Sheridan) falls in love with a prison guard (Pat O'Brien). Red escapes, then tries to give himself up, but gets shot down anyway. "I always wound up dead and never got the girl," he said of his usual roles. "A gangster is never allowed to have any sex life."

O pposite: *Dead End* (1937), a quality Goldwyn production written by Lillian Hellman and directed by William Wyler, was Bogie's best film since *The Petrified Forest*. He delivered a textured performance as "Baby Face" Morton, a gangster who goes home to the slums to see his aging mother and his old flame—a sentimental journey with tragic consequences. Bogie got $3,250 for five weeks of work; Warners made $6,750 for "loaning" him out.

Right: *Crime School* (1938) was Bogie's second film with "the Dead End Kids," a comical troupe of boisterous, mischievous adolescents who mangled the English language with dialogue like "You moidah me! You moidah me!" and went on to make movies of their own. In *Crime School*, Bogie's on the right side of the law, playing the Deputy Commissioner of Correction.

Below: The "hillbilly musical" *Swing Your Lady* (1938) was a career low for Bogie. In this film, which includes such hokey numbers as "Dig Me a Grave in Missouri" and "Mountain Switcheroo," he played a wrestling promoter who manages a dimwitted hulk. He said it was "the worst picture I ever made." Warners had to give him a raise to do it.

Opposite: Busby Berkeley, Warners' resident choreographer known for his kaleidoscopic spectacles of gorgeous girls in elaborate headdresses swishing down staircases, campaigned to direct the romantic farce *Men Are Such Fools* (1938). Bogie, a smarmy radio producer, gets to dance onscreen with Priscilla Lane (shown), although not on a staircase. One reviewer called it "depressingly bad."

Opposite, top: *Angels with Dirty Faces* (1938) combines the surefire elements of the Dead End Kids with Pat O'Brien in uniform (this time as a priest) in yet another tale of how good kids go bad and how others can be saved by their example. Cagney has a famous scenery-chewing scene on his way to execution for killing Bogie.

Above: *Racket Busters* (1938) put Bogie back in the gangster groove, this time as the most powerful racketeer in New York City. "I'm sick to death of being a one-dimensional character," he said. "I have no function except to carry the plot and get killed in the end to prove that virtue is triumphant."

Left: Bogie (left) portrayed gambling cowboy and all-around snake Whip McCord in *The Oklahoma Kid* (1939). Between takes, Bogie ran to the soundstage next door to film *Dark Victory* (1939) with Bette Davis.

Right: In *Dark Victory*, Bogie was cast as an Irish stable hand, complete with brogue, who was hopelessly in love with a rich but dying heiress played by Bette Davis (Sigmund Freud was invited to consult about the psychological aspects but declined). A rare break from Bogie's stereotype, the critics were impressed: "Humphrey Bogart shows that he can act without a gun in his pocket."

Opposite: Bette Davis and Bogie made six movies together. Like him, she began as a B player who fought for better parts and more control over her career. Here, she appears with Joan Crawford and Jack Warner, the studio boss who wrangled with Bogie for seventeen years—but also gave him some of his greatest roles.

Above: Bogart in *You Can't Get Away with Murder* (1939). The title of this movie was also a policy of the Production Code, Hollywood's clumsy attempt to censor itself. Founded after intense pressure from the Catholic Church–backed Legion of Decency, the code targeted sex, profanity, and the glorification of crime, decreeing that no movie murderers could survive. Although started in 1930, the code really took effect in 1934 when Joseph Breen was appointed the official censor of the Motion Pictures Producers and Distributors Association and the head of the "Hays Office," the entity that administered the Production Code.

Above: *The Roaring Twenties* (1939) starring James Cagney had a
good team in producer Hal Wallis, director Raoul Walsh, and
writer Mark Hellinger. But the film and Bogie's role were small
compared to the projects he had to turn down because Warners
wouldn't loan him out: *My Little Chickadee* (the part Bogie wanted
was eventually played by W.C. Fields) and *Of Mice and Men*, which
was later nominated for an Academy Award.

Left: Bogie played a vampire, a role originally intended for Bela Lugosi, in *The Return of Doctor X* (1939). Here, as a dapper—if extremely pale—man-about-town, he steps out for the evening with actress Lya Lys—who would supply him with a long drink before the night was over.

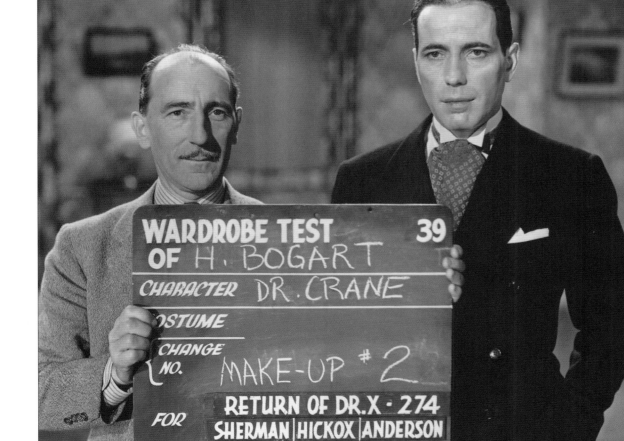

Left: This test helped determine the optimal thickness of blue-white makeup needed to make Bogie a credible living corpse. Bogie was not pleased with his vampire part: "If it'd been...Jack Warner's blood...I wouldn't have minded so much. The trouble was they were drinking mine and I was making this stinking movie."

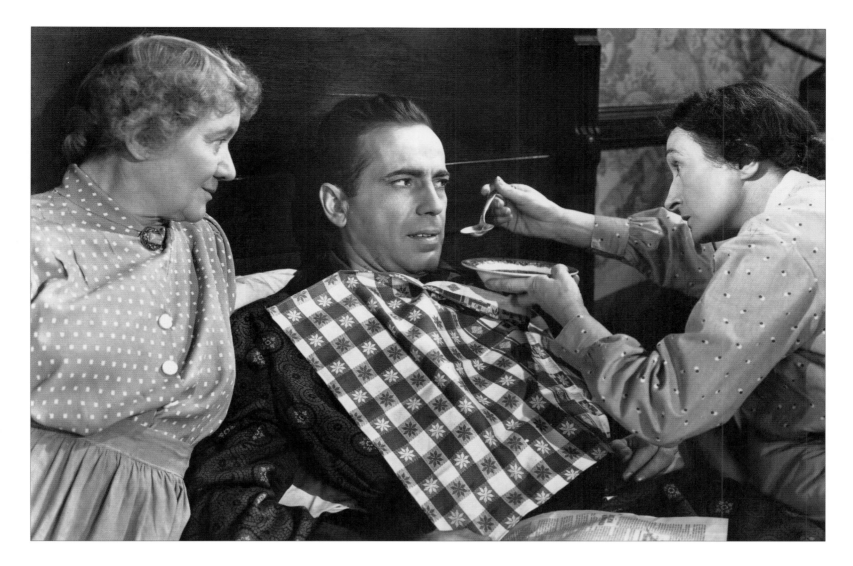

Opposite: In *Invisible Stripes* (1939), Bogie and George Raft play ex-cons who can't find jobs because they served time. Raft, a star rather than a B player, earned $50,000 to Bogie's $10,000 for the picture. The film raised important issues about rehabilitation, but it was a melodrama riddled with clichés. Bogie's last words: "This is it, I guess, and it's okay with me. You can't live forever."

Above: *It All Came True* (1940), produced by Wallis and Hellinger, was an interesting change of pace for Bogie: he played a racketeer who actually does a good deed and lives through the movie. Bogie's character kills a cop with a gun that belongs to Tommy, the son of one of the women who run a boardinghouse. Tommy has to hide to protect himself, so Bogie ends up at the boardinghouse. While holed up there, he is so impressed by the kindness of the women (here, Una O'Connor feeds him soup while he pretends to be sick) that he turns himself in to clear Tommy's name.

Right: Bogie and costar Ida Lupino in *They Drive by Night* (1940). Lupino would also star with Bogie in his next career milestone, *High Sierra*. This would also mark the second and last film Bogie made with George Raft.

Opposite: Mad Dog is on the run, but his gang brings along Marie Garson (Ida Lupino), a drifter who falls for him. At first Earle resists the intrusion of "a dame," but later sacrifices himself to put Marie out of harm's way. This was his most sympathetic gangster to date: a tough guy with a soft center.

Right: Raft refused to play the carnival owner in *The Wagons Roll at Night* (1941), titled to capitalize on the hit *They Drive by Night*. In one fresh touch, Bogie's character, Nick Costner, is killed by a crazed lion that he tried to turn on someone else. On November 23, 1940, the day after the filming ended, Bogie's mother lost her long battle with cancer. "She died as she had lived—with guts," Bogie said.

Below: In *The Maltese Falcon* (1941), a twisted tale of greed, betrayal, and murder, Bogie played detective Sam Spade, who is hired to locate the missing Maltese Falcon statue and who locks horns with villains played by Peter Lorre and Sydney Greenstreet (making his film debut at 357 pounds [162kg]). The film's last line was adapted by Bogie from Shakespeare—he refers to the black bird as "the stuff that dreams are made of."

ight: Sam Spade meets with his former lover and partner's widow, Iva Archer (Gladys George). Spade could have an affair with his partner's wife, yet vow to avenge his partner's death and surrender his own murderous new love over to the police. Spade's paradoxical character made him compelling; Bogie's nuanced portrayal made him unforgettable. The film received an Oscar nomination for Best Picture.

Below: *All Through the Night* (1942), another Raft reject, was a bizarre brew of comedy, crime, and espionage, with Peter Lorre as a Gestapo agent and Phil Silvers and Jackie Gleason in small parts. Bogie, here with Kaaren Verne, plays "Gloves" Donahue, a gambler and Nazi fighter. A successful spoof of the times, it made more money than *Falcon*—which got better reviews.

Opposite, bottom: The winning formula of *High Sierra* was remixed for *The Big Shot* (1942): another prison escape, another mountain hideout, another car chase, and another dame (Irene Manning). The film disappointed Bogie, who expected to get better roles after *Falcon*. In fact, gangster movies had gone out of style when a larger evil—Hitler—arrived, but they came back after the war.

Chapter Four

Out of Africa: Casablanca to the Queen

Opposite: *Casablanca* (1943) was based on a play that sat on a producer's shelf for a year. Originally called *Everybody Comes to Rick's*, it was renamed to evoke the 1939 Charles Boyer hit, *Algiers*. In this publicity still, Bogie (Rick) drinks a toast with Ingrid Bergman (Ilsa, Rick's lost love), and Paul Henreid (Victor Lazlo, Ilsa's husband and the endangered hero).

Above: Bogie and Bergman in *Casablanca*. In their scenes together, Bogie allegedly wore three-inch (7.6cm) wooden blocks tied to his shoes. It was amazing the film turned out as it did. Two weeks before the shooting, they only had one-quarter of the script, which was invented as they went along with everyone contributing ideas. One of Bogie's: "Here's looking at you, kid."

Right: Bogie with Dooley Wilson (Sam) and Sydney Greenstreet (Ferrari). Producer Hal Wallis had considered a female for Sam's role, possibly Lena Horne or Ella Fitzgerald. The famous request was "Play it, Sam"—not "Play it again, Sam," which was Woody Allen's version. "As Time Goes By" was originally written for a 1931 revue of the same name, but its melody and message were perfect for Rick and Ilsa's doomed affair.

Below: Claude Rains, who played the sly Major Renault, had several memorable lines, including "I'm shocked—*shocked* to find that gambling is going on in here!" even as he pockets his own winnings. A cinematic stunner in black and white, the film's dramatic, beautiful shadows are lost in the colorized version.

Above: Ilsa draws on her past with Rick to get him to help her husband. Bergman was concerned she was not beautiful enough for the role. "I look like a milkmaid," she said.

Left: The famous double-fedora scene, in which Rick surrenders his passion for Ilsa to the Cause. Although Warners fought to keep the lovers together, the creative team prevailed. "Miss Bergman is the kind of lady that no man would give up willingly, even to the tune of a lot of high philosophy," Bogie said. "But that was the story and I had to let her slide right out of my arms."

Opposite, top: *Action in the North Atlantic* (1943) was a straight war movie in which Bogie—shown here with Sam Levene, Alan Hale, and Raymond Massey as the wounded captain—cleverly fakes out and destroys a German submarine. By now, Bogie's domestic problems were interfering with his concentration: all the script rewrites he required, together with numerous special effects, helped to drag the film forty-three days behind schedule.

Above: Bogie and the future president of the United States Ronald Reagan with their future ex-wives, Mayo Methot and Jane Wyman.

Right: *Thank Your Lucky Stars* (1943) was a lighthearted showcase of Warners celebrities, who played themselves. This scene, with comedian S.K. "Cuddles" Sakall scolding Bogie, replaced the original idea, which scheduling problems made impossible: Bogie in a zoot suit, singing and dancing with Ida Lupino and Olivia deHavilland as the "Rhythmaniacs."

Right: Desolate Brawley, California, just north of the Mexican border, became North Africa for *Sahara* (1943), a box-office hit in which Bogie leads a stranded and thirsty group of Allies through the desert. During the day, Mayo brought him cold martinis in a thermos; at night, she shouted and broke glass in their room.

Right: In 1944, *Passage to Marseille* (the studio left off the last "s") used *Casablanca* ingredients—Rains, Lorre, Greenstreet, Wallis as producer, and Michael Curtiz as director—but the result was far less dynamic, even with Bogie's single-handed destruction of a German plane. Bogie, ever the antifascist, wanted to do the film because of its unusually frank treatment of French/Nazi collaboration, so Warners used it to bribe him into doing *Conflict*—which he had been refusing to do.

Left: Bogie and Mayo discuss China patterns, circa 1945. Ironically, Bogie played the wife killer in *Conflict* (1945). His costar, Alexis Smith, remembers Bogie as being very troubled and escaping between takes to his chessboard, where he often had three games going at once. Meanwhile, the studio was trying to keep Mayo's problems quiet, steering her to a publicist instead of a psychiatrist for "help."

elow: Bogie and Bacall on the set of *To Have and Have Not* (1944), which was based on the Hemingway novel and filmed in early 1944. The film was directed by Howard Hawks, who "discovered" nineteen-year-old model Lauren Bacall and taught her to make her voice lower and sexier. Bogie also "discovered" Bacall in his own way, but it would take a full year for him to sort himself out and leave Mayo.

Right: "You know how to whistle, don't you, Steve? You just put your lips together...and blow." Bacall demonstrates with the gold whistle he gave her. Although the affair between Bogie and Bacall was obvious, Mayo told *Life* magazine, "In five years we're going to retire and become beachcombers. That is, if Pa can keep his hair and teeth that long." It was supposed to be a jolly remark inspired by Bogie's publicists and her own delusions.

Below: William Faulkner was one of the writers who adapted Raymond Chandler's *The Big Sleep* for the screen. In this 1946 film, Bogie plays Philip Marlowe, a private detective who's hired to trap a blackmailer but gets drawn into a much more complicated plot. This was another Hawks film in which Bacall was "protected" by his tight direction. Without it, she said, "I didn't know what I was doing."

Above: Bogie and Bacall's wedding day—May 21, 1945—capped a year of anguish and failed reconciliations with Mayo, who finally tried rehab in a last attempt to hang onto Bogie. Bacall's first words after the ceremony: "Oh, goodie." Bogie remained friendly with his first two wives, but had no further contact with Mayo—though she told the press, "Bogie and I are the best of friends....It was a very pleasant marriage."

Right: *Dark Passage* (1947) spawned the television series *The Fugitive* as well as the 1993 film of the same name. Framed for his wife's murder, Vincent Parry (Bogie) goes after the real killer while being pursued by police, undergoing plastic surgery to disguise himself. The character's face is hidden with unusual camera angles until after the surgery, when he emerges looking exactly like Humphrey Bogart. Bacall plays Irene Jansen, a woman who gives a stranger (Parry) a ride, comes to believe in his innocence, and ends up falling in love with him.

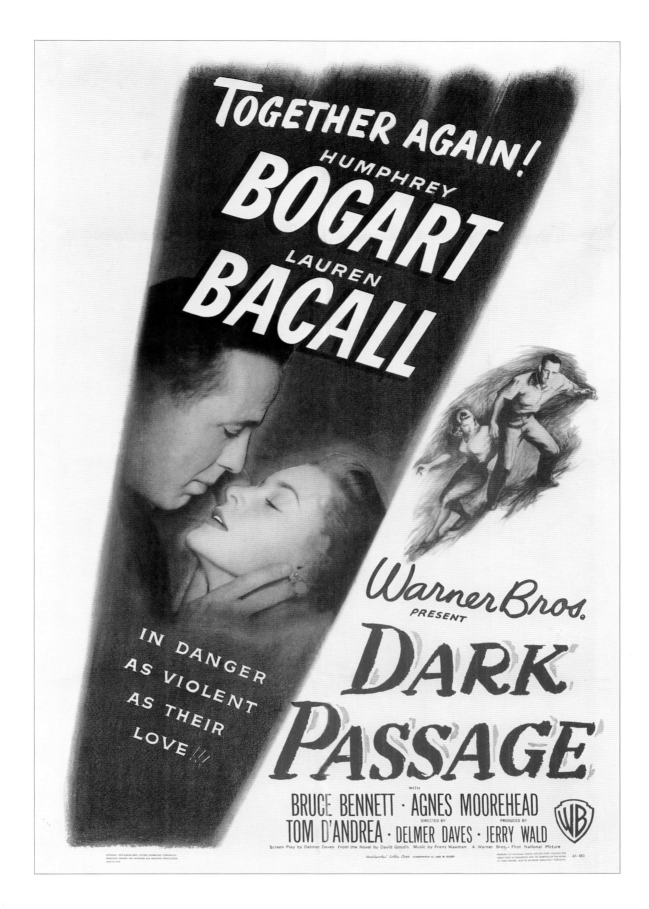

A bove: While shooting *Dark Passage*, Bogie's career moved further into the light. He negotiated a sixty-seven-page contract—the longest ever for any actor in 1947—with script and director approval and $200,000 for one picture a year. "It was take it or leave it," reported the *Herald-Tribune*. "The studio took it. Bogart and Jack Warner shook hands...and agreed that henceforth they would love each other like brothers."

Above: Bogie absorbed in a chess match on the set of *Dead Reckoning* (1947). He often played chess by mail with his old friends in New York. Few people knew his intellectual side—the Bogie who subscribed to the *Harvard Law Review* and quoted Plato, Emerson, and Shakespeare.

Opposite: At the peak of his career, Bogie underwent the traditional Hollywood hand- and foot-printing in front of Grauman's Chinese Theater. Bogie, shown here with Sid Grauman and Bacall, wrote in the cement, "Sid, may you never die until I kill you." Bogie's humor could be a little confrontational: on meeting Sinatra, he said, "I hear you've got a voice that makes girls faint. Make me faint."

ight: Postwar paranoia inspired the House Un-American Activities Committee (HUAC), which spent ten years hunting Communists. Many Hollywood people, working behind and in front of the camera, were dragged before the HUAC to "confess" their leftist leanings or implicate their friends. Bogie and Bacall were part of a committee that stormed Washington in October 1947 in order to protest the witch hunt. Also present were John Huston (seventh from left), Paul Henreid (center), and Danny Kaye (fifth from right), among other celebrities.

I'M NO COMMUNIST

Left: Anyone "blacklisted" by the HUAC was denied Hollywood employment. While Bogie was originally defiant, the combination of studio and media pressure—and the abrupt loss of financial backing for his producer friend Mark Hellinger—forced him to publicly declare that his Washington trip had been "ill advised, even foolish." This picture in *Photoplay* magazine was supposed to reassure the public that Bogie wasn't "a Red."

Opposite: *The Two Mrs. Carrolls* (1947) was inspired by *Conflict* and filmed shortly after. Once again Bogie's character plans to murder his wife to marry a beautiful younger woman (played by Alexis Smith in both films). Here, he struggles with Barbara Stanwyck after she refuses to drink her poisoned milk.

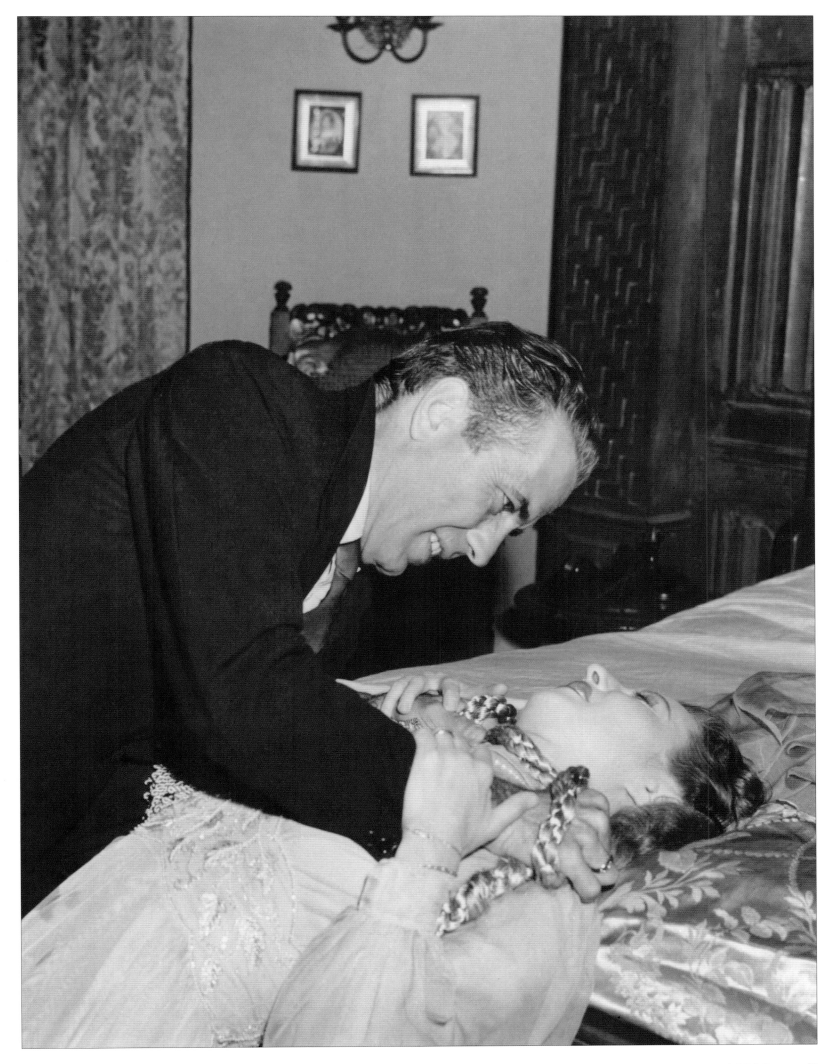

Right: Finally, another plum role: the sleazy prospector Fred C. Dobbs in *The Treasure of the Sierra Madre* (1948), written and directed by John Huston—who won Oscars for both his contributions. It was one of the first American movies to be made elsewhere (Mexico). Many consider both the film and performance Bogie's best, but it bombed at the box office. "Critical praise doesn't pay the bills," Bogie said.

Below: Bogie and Bacall on *Santana*, where Bogie spent forty-five weekends a year. "An actor needs something to stabilize his personality, something to nail down what he really is, not what he is currently pretending to be," he said. "Hemingway said the sea was the last free place in the world, and I respect it and love it."

eft: *Key Largo* (1948) is the story of hostages held in a small Florida seaside hotel. Tightly directed by John Huston, it contained memorable performances by Edward G. Robinson as the flamboyant gangster Johnny Rocco; John Barrymore as the crusty, wheelchair-bound proprietor; Bogie as the wry, reluctant hero Frank McCloud; and a brief film debut by Jay Silverheels, who later became the Lone Ranger's "faithful Indian companion," Tonto. Huston had to literally twist Bacall's arm to get some genuine emotion out of her. (Huston's techniques were often unconventional: he once tweaked Bogie's nose and made Mary Astor run around the set of *The Maltese Falcon* to make her breathless.)

bove: *Key Largo* was Bogie's fifth movie with Robinson. Although Robinson's character, Johnny Rocco, is a cold-blooded killer, he is frightened by the hurricane that hits the hotel. As the defiant good guy, McCloud sneers at Rocco's cowardice and suggests, "If it doesn't stop, shoot it." Despite his crude face and rough movie persona, Robinson (born Emmanuel Goldenberg in Romania) was actually a courtly and cultured man who spoke several languages.

Opposite: Bogie and Huston share a welcome laugh while filming a tense story. Bogie and Huston were pals; actress Evelyn Keyes, Huston's wife, said, "They acted like a couple of kids all the time." Their famous drinking inspired the notion, during one merry evening at the Hustons', to play football in the living room—using a Ming vase as the ball. The final score: Kids 1, Ming 0.

Above: In 1947, Bogie formed his own film company, Santana Productions, hoping to showcase new talent. In Santana's first effort, *Knock on Any Door* (1949), Bogie plays a lawyer defending a young cop killer (John Derek). Bogie is shown here opposite actress Susan Perry. The film contained the famous advice "Live fast, die young, and leave a good-looking corpse."

Right: Santana's second film also made money. *Tokyo Joe* (1949) borrowed elements from both *Casablanca* and *Across the Pacific*, with Bogie as Joe Barrett, an ex–fighter pilot who owns a night-club. Here, he rescues his ex-wife's kidnapped daughter (Laura Lee Michael). A few days into filming, Bogie finally became a father him-self with the arrival of his son, Stephen Humphrey Bogart, on January 6, 1949.

Above: In September 1949, Bogie and pal Bill Seeman brought two twenty-two-pound (10kg) stuffed pandas to posh El Morocco as their late-night "dates." When someone tried to snatch his, Bogie allegedly shoved her away, saying, "I'm a happily married man—don't touch my panda!" The judge dismissed the assault charge, ruling that Bogie had properly defended his property. Here, outside the courthouse, he's escorted past his fans.

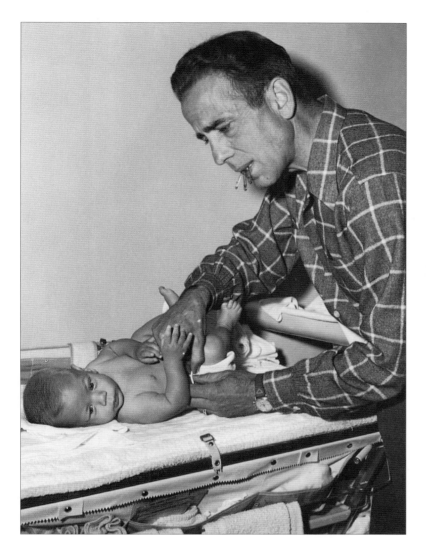

Below: After the creative peaks of *Sierra Madre* and *Key Largo*, *Chain Lightning* (1950) was flat. Bogie plays test pilot Matt Brennan, shown here emerging from a new escape device. The combination of dull assignments and the studio's refusal to help with the panda incident heightened Bogie's determination to break free of Warners for good.

Above: Bogie in an uncharacteristic situation: out of his depth. The wording of this 1949 press release indicates that Hollywood found it remarkable for a "tough guy" to diaper a baby. In fact, Bogie was awkward with his small children and believed he wouldn't live to see them grow up, when they'd "finally have something to say to each other." Sadly, he was right.

Right: Santana's third film, *In a Lonely Place* (1950), was one of the best Bogie films ever made. Bogie played screenwriter Dixon Steele, a character much like himself—intelligent, caustic, funny, alcoholic, troubled in his relationships with women, and given to unexpected anger. Bogie never liked the film; perhaps it was too close to his private self. "He was a guy who didn't open up much," said a friend. Bogie wanted Bacall to play the part of Laurel Gray, the woman Steele loves but drives away with his violence, but Warners refused to loan Bacall out. Their intent was probably to punish Bogie for his growing independence, but it resulted in driving him even further away.

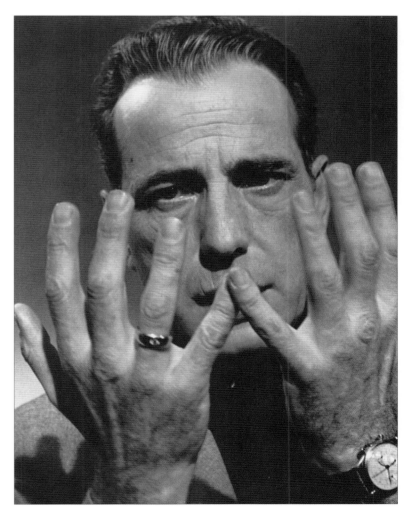

Above: *The Enforcer* (1951) was Bogie's last movie under contract with Warners. It had interesting plot twists and characters, including a strong Zero Mostel as larcenous Big Babe Lazich. Here, Bogie as Assistant D.A. Martin Ferguson strains to rescue escaping prisoner Joseph Rico (Ted De Corsia), who witnessed a murder and is afraid he'll be killed in jail. With this stunt, he saves them the trouble.

Right: Bogie in *Sirocco* (1951), Santana's fourth film: "It was one we had to do. It stank, of course." Although the acting was good, *Sirocco* suffered from one of Santana's main weaknesses—the lack of a veteran support crew. Another problem was insufficient clout and money to compete with the major studios for the best properties and stars.

Above: On the set of *The African Queen* (1951), with Hepburn, Bogie, Bacall, and Huston. The studio first considered Charles Laughton and Elsa Lancaster; then David Niven and Bette Davis. Hepburn fell ill during the filming, losing twenty pounds (9kg) from her already thin frame, but Bogie was spared: "All I ate was baked beans, canned asparagus, and Scotch whiskey. Whenever a fly bit Huston or me, it dropped dead."

Left: A thoroughly misleading ad for Bogie's most beloved movie and his own favorite, *The African Queen*, a timeless story of adventure, patriotism, and slow-dawning love. The studios had difficulty imagining a romance between a middle-aged spinster and a drunken sailor; an RKO reader, reflecting the limited mentality of the time, said, "Both are physically unattractive, and their love scenes...are distasteful and not a little disgusting."

Left: Rose Sayer (Hepburn) inspects Charlie Allnut (Bogie) and his latest collection of river hazards. On location in the Belgian Congo, the cast and crew suffered intense heat and humidity, foul water, biting insects, scorpions, poisonous snakes, dysentery, and malaria. At least the leeches were fake—director John Huston wanted Bogie to use real ones, but he refused.

Below: Drafted into battle and surprised into love, Allnut was Bogie's ultimate hesitant hero. Famous lines include: "You crazy, psalm-singing, skinny old maid!" "I never dreamed that any mere physical experience could be so...stimulating." "Nature, Mr. Allnut, is what we are put in this world to rise above." "I now pronounce you man and wife. Proceed with the execution!"

Opposite: Bogie finally meets Oscar in 1952 for his performance in *The African Queen*. His Best Actor award was presented by Claire Trevor in 1948. Bogie had just planned to say "It's about time!" and walk off the stage, but according to friend Richard Brooks, "He kisses the broad, they throw the Oscar at him, and he looks over, tears in his eyes, and thanks about forty people....John [Huston] he thanked *nine* times."

Chapter Five

The Last Ten

Opposite: In 1952, Bogie had it all: a flourishing family and career, good friends, and his yacht, *Santana*, which he raced to numerous championships. After daughter Leslie's birth in August, Bacall moved the family to a white brick mansion in Holmby Hills. Bogie, born into money and cynical about high society, said, "We moved where all the creeps live." But he liked some of his neighbors, especially Judy Garland. Bogie did a cameo in her 1954 movie *A Star Is Born*—an off-camera, "drunken" request for her character to sing "Melancholy Baby."

Above: In *Deadline U.S.A.* (1952), Bogie played a crusading editor fighting for a free press and against a notorious gangster. Director Richard Brooks noted Bogie's fatigue and irritability: "It was totally unlike him. Plenty was wrong."

Above: Bogie with Bacall and Marilyn Monroe, who had just filmed *How to Marry a Millionaire* (1953). Bogie, who was officially "not a bosom man," was nonetheless momentarily interested in Monroe's famous attributes. "Bogie wanted a woman who was as arrogant and tough as a man," Bacall wrote. On September 23, 1953, soon after this picture was released, Bogie finally ended his seventeen-year association with Warners—and bought out Bacall's contract as well.

Right: *Battle Circus* (1953) was "embarrassingly bad," with no chemistry between doctor Bogie and nurse June Allyson. Once again, Bogie's career peak was followed by a slump. He lost two good roles: the lead in *Come Back, Little Sheba* (1952), a milestone for Burt Lancaster; and the role of the veteran fisherman in Hemingway's *The Old Man and the Sea* (1958), which Spencer Tracy played so memorably after Bogie's death.

Above: In *The Barefoot Contessa* (1954), Bogart played Harry Dawes, a cynical ex–movie director who befriends the beautiful doomed Maria Vargas (Ava Gardner). Bogie disapproved of Gardner, who was separated from his friend Frank Sinatra and busy having an affair with a bullfighter at the time: "Half the world's female population would throw themselves at Frank's feet, and here you are flouncing around with guys who wear capes and little ballerina slippers!"

Above: *The Caine Mutiny* (1954) gave Bogie his last great role—the disintegrating Captain Queeg (on deck here with Robert Francis). Bogie lost the Oscar to Marlon Brando that year, but won the Golden Lion at the Venice Film Festival for his nuanced, controlled, sympathetic portrayal of a man destroyed by his own paranoia. It was Bogie's idea for Queeg to obsessively butter his toast as a clue to his fragile state of mind.

COURT IN SESSION

COURT MEMBERS ONLY

Above: Someone asked Bogie how he managed that deranged look in the close-ups. "Easy," he grinned. "I'm nuts, you know." Playing the defeated Queeg was also easy for Bogie, who was tired and plagued by a persistent cough. Meanwhile, Bogie sold Santana Productions to Columbia for $1 million in December 1954.

bove: Santana bought the rights to *Beat the Devil* (1954), a quirky, comical movie about shipwrecks, buried uranium, and selling vacuum cleaners in Kenya. With Gina Lollabrigida (shown), whom Bogie called "Low Bridge," Peter Lorre, Robert Morley, and Jennifer Jones, the film was Santana's last. It was also a critical success, a box-office dud, and a cult hit.

Below: On location in Ravello, Italy. *Beat the Devil* was Huston's and Bogie's last film together; they attempted *The Man Who Would Be King*, but the logistics never worked (it was made in 1975 with Sean Connery and Michael Caine). After the Production Office rejected Huston's original script for having too much kissing and not enough punishment for criminals, Truman Capote was brought in to fix it.

Opposite: Bogie never wanted to play a Wall Street tycoon (Cary Grant was director Wilder's first choice), but ended up in *Sabrina* (1954) anyway. His chemistry with Audrey Hepburn was leaden; he had a longstanding dislike of right-wing costar William Holden (the feelings were mutual); and he thought Hepburn and Holden's affair was unprofessional. "This picture is a crock of crap," Bogie said.

Above: *The Desperate Hours* (1955) featured another hostage situation like those in *The Petrified Forest* and *Key Largo*, with Bogie and fellow escapees Dewey Martin and Robert Middleton terrorizing a family. Scenes filmed outside the house lessened the tension: Paul Newman, who had Bogie's role on Broadway, said of those scenes, "That whole sense of confinement and oppression was lost."

eft: Despite his failing health, Bogie had his busiest year in 1955. Right after Bogie finished *Hours*, he started *The Left Hand of God* (1955), playing an American flyer forced down in China who impersonates a priest and falls for a nurse—portrayed by the lovely and delicate Gene Tierney. Tierney was on the verge of a breakdown during the filming, and Bogie talked with her each day, encouraging her to get help. "His patience and understanding carried me through the film," she later said.

elow: *We're No Angels* (1955) was a comedy about three escaped convicts who play guardian angels to a family of shopkeepers. (From left: Aldo Ray, Bogie, and Peter Ustinov.) Bogie insisted that actress Joan Bennett play the mother; she had not worked in three years because of a family scandal. "He made the stand [against] the underground movement to stamp me out," Bennett said.

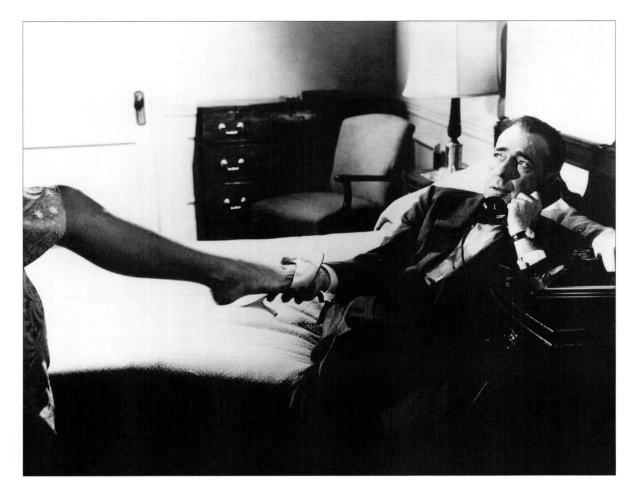

Left: Bogie's last film was *The Harder They Fall* (1956), which contains some of the most realistic boxing footage ever shot. Bogie played Eddie Willis, a fight promoter who challenges syndicate head Nick Benko (Rod Steiger). Steiger used the new Method technique, which Bogie called "the scratch-your-ass-and-mumble-school-of-acting." Despite their differences, Steiger remembers "his independence and professionalism and his kindness to me."

Left: The Bogarts in 1955, with Bogie already looking in another direction. In January 1956 he was finally persuaded to see a doctor for his eating difficulties and his thirty-minute coughing fits. By then the cancer had spread so far that they immediately removed his esophagus, two lymph nodes, and a rib, and reattached his stomach. By all reports he never complained; even as his body dwindled to eighty pounds his spirit remained strong. Bogie died on January 14, 1957. His ashes rest in the Garden of Memory at Forest Lawn, far from his beloved Pacific Ocean where he wanted them to be.

Opposite: In July 1997, Bogie joined Marilyn Monroe and James Dean in the U.S. Postal Service's Legends of Hollywood series of commemorative stamps. Son Stephen is a television producer, daughter Leslie a yoga therapist—and the only one of Bogie's surviving family not to write a book about him.

Conclusion

Bogie is a legend—the number one movie legend of all time, according to *Entertainment Weekly*. Like Marilyn and Elvis, he died too young and will never grow old. But this doesn't explain why *Casablanca* is one of the most frequently aired movies on television. Nor does the intriguing overlap between Bogie's screen and "real" selves, since most of his current fans have no idea who he actually was. His trademark "Hey, shweetheart" is imitated by people who weren't even born in his lifetime.

It's more likely that Bogie's lasting appeal lies in his complexity, which was so different from the cardboard figures on celluloid today. Unlike the Terminator or James Bond, Sam Spade and Rick could be hurt—and showed it when they were. Bogie's heroes were hesitant, his villains conflicted. Far from polar opposites, they nearly met in the middle: each a flawed human being, capable of both nobility and evil, and struggling with choices. In Bogie's brilliant portrayal of Captain Queeg, he gave us a fierce madman who is also terrified by his own madness. Even his thugs had the touch of the gentleman about them, along with a whiff of weary sadness—as if they, too, had expected more of themselves.

Not flashy, not handsome, wearing his own clothes rather than relying on studio style, Bogie managed to project the steady flame of strength held in reserve, of high cards not played. "I stick my neck out for nobody," Rick says—twice—in *Casablanca*, but we know Bogie's personal code will force him into action, just as it does in *The Maltese Falcon*, *The African Queen*, and many of his best movies. There were no psychobabbling soliloquies for Bogie, no computer-generated pyrotechnics to heighten the drama—the action was the flash in his dark eyes, his smoldering gaze, and that trademark pull of his mouth. He was his own special effect and it was more than enough.

Bogie's life was not an easy one, and he was often as contradictory as his characters. Generous and loyal, he also enjoyed needling people; an admitted physical coward, he put his career on the line for political causes; a high-school dropout, he was a master at chess. There was always the sense of a real person behind his movie persona, someone wrestling with fear and courage, weighted with a history of tender hopes and bitter disappointments.

So perhaps this is the key to Bogie's enduring legend: he was just enough hero to admire from afar, and just enough regular guy to recognize up close. Both fantasy and familiar, he helps us believe that we, too, would do The Right Thing in a crisis. And so we identify with him, root for him, count on him—and continue to love him.

O pposite: *Across the Pacific* (1942) was Bogie's best war movie. Directed by John Huston (until he got drafted), it reunited Bogie with Mary Astor as well as Sydney Greenstreet, who plays Dr. Lorenz, a Japanese sympathizer. Bogie pretends to be a dishonorably discharged army vet on the make but is actually a secret agent after Lorenz. His character, Rick Leland, is another study in shadows and light, preparing the creative ground for his next turn as Rick— the role that would vault him into legend.

A bove: Bogart in *Conflict* (1945). Clad in trench coat and fedora, he displays the classic Bogie look.

Filmography

Broadway's Like That, 1930.

A Devil With Women, 1930.

Up the River, 1930.

Body and Soul, 1931.

Bad Sister, 1931.

Women of All Nations, 1931.

A Holy Terror, 1931.

Love Affair, 1932.

Big City Blues, 1932.

Three on a Match, 1932.

Midnight, 1934.

The Petrified Forest, 1936.

Bullets or Ballots, 1936.

Two Against the World, 1936.

China Clipper, 1936.

Isle of Fury, 1936.

Black Legion, 1937.

The Great O'Malley, 1937.

Marked Woman, 1937.

Kid Galahad, 1937.

San Quentin, 1937.

Dead End, 1937.

Stand In, 1937.

Swing Your Lady, 1938.

Crime School, 1938.

Men Are Such Fools, 1938.

The Amazing Dr. Clitterhouse, 1938.

Racket Rumors, 1938.

Angels With Dirty Faces, 1938.

King of the Underworld, 1939.

The Oklahoma Kid, 1939.

Dark Victory, 1939.

You Can't Get Away With Murder, 1939.

The Roaring Twenties, 1939.

The Return of Doctor X, 1939.

Invisible Stripes, 1939.

Virginia City, 1940.

It All Came True, 1940.

Brother Orchid, 1940.

They Drive By Night, 1940.

High Sierra, 1941.

The Wagons Roll At Night, 1941.

The Maltese Falcon, 1941.

All Through the Night, 1942.

The Big Shot, 1942.

Across the Pacific, 1942.

Casablanca, 1943.

Action in the North Atlantic, 1943.

Thank Your Lucky Stars, 1943.

Sahara, 1943.

Passage to Marseille, 1944.

Report from the Front, 1944.

To Have and Have Not, 1944.

Conflict, 1945.

Hollywood Victory Caravan, 1945.

Two Guys From Milwaukee, 1946.

The Big Sleep, 1946.

Dead Reckoning, 1947.

The Two Mrs. Carrolls, 1947.

Dark Passage, 1947.

Always Together, 1948.

The Treasure of the Sierra Madre, 1948.

Key Largo, 1948.

Knock on Any Door, 1949.

Tokyo Joe, 1949.

Chain Lightening, 1950.

In a Lonely Place, 1950.

The Enforcer, 1951.

Sirocco, 1951.

The African Queen, 1951.

Deadline USA, 1952.

Battle Circus, 1953.

Beat the Devil, 1954.

The Caine Mutiny, 1954.

Sabrina, 1954.

The Barefoot Contessa, 1954.

We're No Angels, 1955.

The Left Hand of God, 1955.

The Desperate Hours, 1955.

The Harder They Fall, 1956.

Bibliography

Bacall, Lauren. *By Myself.* New York: Random House, 1978.

Bogart, Stephen Humphrey (with Gary Provost). *Bogart: In Search of My Father.* New York: Penguin Books, 1996.

Koch, Howard. *Casablanca: Script and Legend.* New York: Overlook Press, 1973.

Meyers, Jeffrey. *Bogart: A Life in Hollywood.* New York: Houghton Mifflin Company, 1997.

Sperber. A.M., and Lax, Eric. *Bogart.* New York: William Morrow and Company, Inc., 1997.

Photography Credits

Archive Photos: pp. 51 bottom, 58, 79; Michael Barson Collection: p. 68 bottom; Darlene Hammond Collection: p. 77 bottom; Universal: p. 24

Corbis-Bettmann: pp. 20, 74

Everett Collection: pp. 36, 64 top, 75 top left, 82 top

The Kobal Collection: pp. 2, 55, 63 top, 65, 71 left, 80, 87

Courtesy Museum of Modern Art: pp. 6, 8, 9, 10, 11, 13, 15, 16, 17 right, 18, 22 top, 25 top, 26 both, 27, 28, 29, 31 top, 32, 33 both, 34, 35 top and bottom left, 37 bottom, 38, 39, 40 bottom, 42, 43 both, 44 top, 45, 46, 47 bottom, 48, 49 both, 50, 51 top, 52 both, 53, 54, 56 top, 57 both, 59 both, 60 bottom, 60-61 top, 62, 63 bottom, 64 bottom, 66, 67, 69, 70 bottom, 72, 73 both, 75 top right and bottom, 76 top, 77 top, 78 both, 81, 82 bottom, 83, 84, 85, 86 both, 88, 89 both, 90 both, 92, 93

Photofest: pp. 14, 17 left, 21, 22 bottom, 23, 35 bottom, 30, 31 bottom, 25 bottom right, 37 top, 40 top, 41, 44 bottom, 47 top, 56 bottom, 61 bottom, 70 top, 71 right, 76 bottom

©Reuters/Fred Prouser/Archive Photos: p. 91

UPI/Corbis-Bettmann: pp. 19, 68 top

Index